Sticky Notes Haiku

Also by Robert Epstein:

A Congregation of Cows: Moo Haiku

A Walk around Spring Lake: Haiku

(Editor) *All the Way Home: Aging in Haiku*

(Editor) *Beyond the Grave: Contemporary Afterlife Haiku*

Checkout Time is Noon: Death Awareness Haiku

Checkout Time is Soon: More Death Awareness Haiku

(Editor) *Dreams Wander On: Contemporary Poems of Death Awareness*

(Co-Editor with Miriam Wald) *Every Chicken, Cow, Fish and Frog: Animal Rights Haiku*

Free to Dance Forever: Mourning Haiku for My Mother

Haiku Days of Remembrance: In Honor of My Father

Haiku Edge: New and Selected Poems

Haiku Forest Afterlife

Healing into Haiku: On Illness and Pain

(Second author with Stacy Taylor) *Living Well with a Hidden Disability*

Nothing is Empty: A Whole Haiku World

(Editor) *Now This: Contemporary Poems of Beginnings, Renewals, and Firsts*

Poor Robert's Almanac: Little Observations on Life

(With Stacy Taylor) *Suffering Buddha: The Zen Way Beyond Health and Illness*

(Editor) *The Breath of Surrender: A Collection of Recovery-Oriented Haiku*

(Editor) *The Helping Hand Haiku Anthology*

(Compiler with Sherry Phillips) *The Natural Man: A Thoreau Anthology*

Reckoning with Winter: A Haiku Hailstorm

(Editor) *The Sacred in Contemporary Haiku*

(Editor) *The Signature Haiku Anthology (Including Senryu and Tanka)*

(Editor) *The Temple Bell Stops: Contemporary Poems of Grief, Loss and Change*

(Editor) *They Gave Us Life: Celebrating Mothers, Fathers & Others in Haiku*

Turkey Heaven: Animal Rights Haiku Turning the Page to Old: Haiku & Senryu

Sticky Notes Haiku:
This Life

Robert Epstein

Middle Island Press
2020

ISBN 978-1-7341254-8-1

Middle Island Press
PO Box 354
West Union, WV 26456

Courage – you develop courage by doing small things like just as if you wouldn't want to pick up a 100-pound weight without preparing yourself.

~ Maya Angelou

Don't be afraid to give your best to what are seemingly small jobs.

~ Dale Carnegie

One sees great things from the valley; only small things from the peak.

~ Gilbert K. Chesterton

A mighty flame followeth a tiny spark.

~ Dante

Truth is so excellent that if it praises but small things they become excellent.

~ Leonardo da Vinci

An orator of times past declared that his calling was to make small things appear to be grand.

~ Michel de Montaigne

If you take care of the small things, the big things take care of themselves.

~ Emily Dickinson

Great things are not done by impulse but by a series of small things brought together.

~ George Eliot

He that despiseth small things will perish little by little.

~ Ralph Waldo Emerson

There are many things that seem improbable only so long as one does not attempt them.

~ *André Gide*

Most people would succeed in small things if they were not troubled with great ambitions.

~ *Henry Wadsworth Longfellow*

. . . [O]ne must not withdraw from the task if he has some small things to offer — he does so at the risk of diminishing his own humanity.

~ *Bernard Malamud*

The habit of attending to small things and of appreciating small courtesies is one of the important marks of a good person.

~ *Nelson Mandela*

Perfection is no small thing, but it is made up of small things.

~ *Michelangelo*

These small things – nutrition, place, recreation, the whole casuistry of selfishness – are inconceivably more important than everything one has taken to be important so far.

~ *Friedrich Nietzsche*

We fought so long against small things that we became small ourselves.

~ *Eugene O'Neill*

For the person for whom small things do not exist, the great is not great.

~ *José Ortega y Gasset*

Little things console us because little things afflict us.

~Blaise Pascal

Do one thing everyday that scares you. Those small things that make us uncomfortable help us build courage to do the work we do.

~Eleanor Roosevelt

Be faithful in small things because it is in them that your strength lies.

~Mother Teresa

Great things are done by a series of small things brought together.

~Vincent Van Gogh

Success in life is founded upon attention to the small things rather than to the large things; to the everyday things nearest to us rather than to the things that are remote and uncommon.

~Booker T. Washington

Dedicated to. . .

Natalie Goldberg

Table of Contents

Acknowledgments

I am always happy to express appreciation for family and friends: Louise and Mel Adler, Janet Amptman, Kathy DiNapoli, Kim Durham, David J. and Nancy Eagle, Debbie Edwards, Martin Epstein, Clara Knopfler, Joy McCall, Alyson and Anthony Nicolosi, Sherry Phillips, Judy Rader, Katherine Raine, Rocco Randazzo, David H. Rosen, Wendy Etsuko Siu, Lillian Schwartz, Joan Vander Ryk, CarrieAnn Thunell, Kathy Waters and Erika Zarco. Jay Schlesinger, Sophie Soltani, Stacy Taylor and Miriam Wald—in whom I have confided for so many years—deserve my deepest gratitude. I also want to give special thanks to Jay for discussing with me aspects of the book as it was taking shape.

I learned a few weeks ago that one of my most respected supervisors, Dan B. Wile, died back in March of this year. I was profoundly saddened by the news of his passing, as he was a therapy genius who developed his own therapy approach to working with couples. I pay tribute to Dan in one of the poems in these pages. And, in searching online for an article written by a transpersonal psychologist, John Welwood, I was shocked to discover that he, too, had died last year at the age of 75. I wish to acknowledge here my debt of gratitude to both of these dedicated mental health professionals with long and distinguished careers.

Thirty years ago, I found a copy of Natalie Goldberg's book, *Writing Down the Bones*. It couldn't have come at a more crucial time because I had a crisis of faith as a new mental health professional struggling with debilitating self-doubt. I lived through many dark nights of the soul, writing in the Zen spirit of Natalie's book and reached a point of liberation that enabled me to renew my commitment to the helping professions. I am eternally grateful to Natalie, and dedicate this book to her. A prolific writer, Natalie's subsequent books continue to be a great inspiration to me.

With ever-deepening gratitude, I want to acknowledge Christina Taylor of Middle Island Press for all her help in bringing this poetry collection to print.

Preface

In life what matters most, sticks.

~*Anonymous*

Maybe sticky notes have gone out of style and I don't know it. I could be living an old-fashioned life. Anything I write starts out on paper; I don't use my Smart phone for reminders because I don't have a Smart phone; I have a dumb flip phone, and I am fine with that.

While sheltering in place due to the novel coronavirus pandemic, I have had plenty of time to observe my habits. I like to write notes to myself, lots of them. Some are on small, colored sheets of paper and some are on post-its or sticky notes. In fact, I have a pop-up sticky note dispenser on my night stand in case I wake up and want to record a haiku or dream. I attach them to the underside of a tissue box that is also on the night stand. It's a strange habit, yet it works at 3 or 4 in the morning.

Why a book about sticky notes? Because, like most things, sticky notes are emblematic. We stick them on the computer, on the refrigerator, on the mirror, on the car dashboard. If we're not careful, they can end up everywhere like ants after the rains. That makes them ubiquitous, at the very least, and maybe even significant. Our lives, from a certain perspective, are encapsulated by them. Focusing on sticky notes is one with Vincent Van Gough, who made a point of saying, "I'll start with small things."

What is the significance of small things? I invite you to contemplate this important question. I will also share with you what a poet, a religious woman and a Jewish mystic have said about small things. First, the poet, Rainer Maria Rilke:

> If you trust in Nature, in the small Things that hardly anyone sees and that so suddenly can become huge, immeasurable; if you have this love for what is humble and try very simply, as someone who serves, to win the confidence of what seems poor, then everything will become easier.

Mother Teresa, who dedicated her life to serving the poor and sought out what was hard, not easy, has this to say about the integral relationship between what is humble or small and what is significant or great:

> We must not drift away from humble works, because these are the works that nobody will do. It is never too small. We are so small we look at things in a small way. But God, being Almighty, sees everything great. Therefore, even if you write a letter for a blind man or you just go sit and listen, or you take the mail for him, or you visit somebody or bring a flower to somebody — small things — or wash clothes for somebody, or clean the house. Very humble work, that is where you and I must be. For there are many people who can do big things. But there are very few people who will do the small things.

Even more succinctly, Mother Teresa said strongly and eloquently: "I don't do great things. I do small things with great love." The founder of the Catholic Order of the Missionaries of Charity in Calcutta, she also observed: "The ocean is made of drops."

Abraham Joshua Heschel was a 20th century Jewish theologian who grasped the connection between small things and the divine, which Mother Teresa pointed to. Here is what he realized:

> Awe is what enables us to see in the world intimations of the divine, to sense in small things the beginning of infinite significance, to sense the ultimate in the common and the simple, to feel in the rush of the passing the stillness of the eternal.

We want to stick to things; we also want things to stick to — or *by* — us. That strikes me as noteworthy. In our quest for permanence, the post-it is an oxymoronic combination of permanent and impermanent, which makes it all the more intriguing as a source of poetic inspiration. Call me eccentric, but I seek realization the ordinary. . . that which is barely noticeable. Post-its may be everywhere but that can render them almost invisible. The great mystery of life is embedded right here if only we are alert enough to follow the spider silk to the infinite. It is where we all end up, sooner or later. Will you have a look with me?

Most of all, I implore the reader to remember what T. S. Eliot, writing in the *Four Quartets*, brilliantly understood:

We shall not cease exploration
And the end of all our exploring
Will be to arrive where we started
And know the place for the first time.

Afterword

vincent tripi, a Buddhist-oriented poet I greatly respect, rightly highlights in *call it haiku*[1] the importance of place in haiku. I suspect this is the case because all of us long to be rooted *somewhere* in time and place. Too, all life is happening in this place at this time. As someone whose life was shattered when my father uprooted the family because he got a new job in another state, I found myself searching for decades to recover a sense of home. Of course, there was no going back to my beloved childhood home in Saddle Brook, NJ. It finally dawned on me that home is not in any given location but in one's heart. I have breathed more easily ever since. So, while I agree that place matters in haiku, this brief form of Japanese poetry also *transcends* place. Look for poetry in the revelation of truth, for truth is a thread that moves from the small to the great; the finite to the infinite; from words to the silence beyond.

Notes

1. vincent tripi. *call it haiku.* Windsor, CT: bottle rockets press with tribe press, 2018.

Robert Epstein
El Cerrito, CA
26 July 2020

Sticky Notes Haiku

When everything is significant,

we are in the haiku place.

~ vincent tripi, *call it haiku*

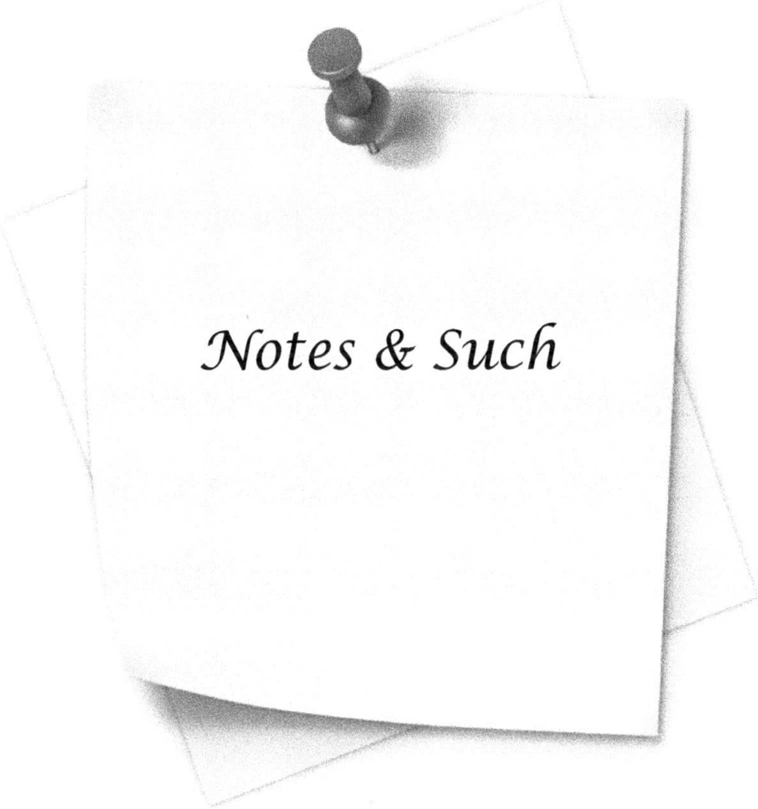

Notes & Such

a clean post-it
what will you
write?

dappled yet plenty of room for three lines

in lieu
of my memory more
sticky notes now

past midnight —
dreams that come
in scribbles

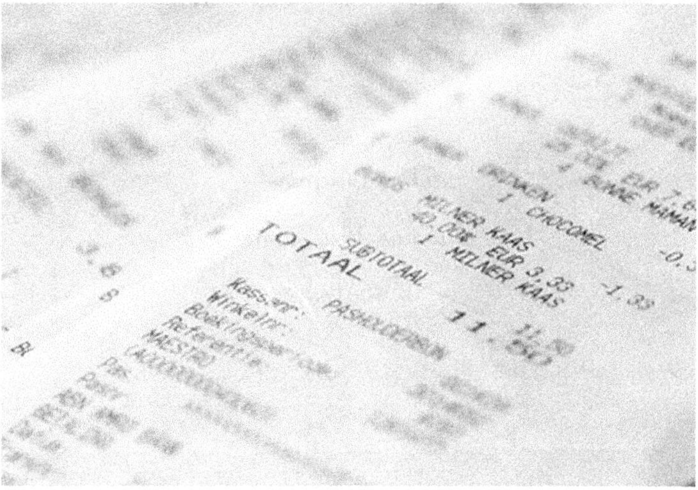
1 CHOCOMEL
MILNER KAAS
1 MILNER KAAS
SUBTOTAAL
TOTAAL

went to the store...
her bookmark dated
7/5/83

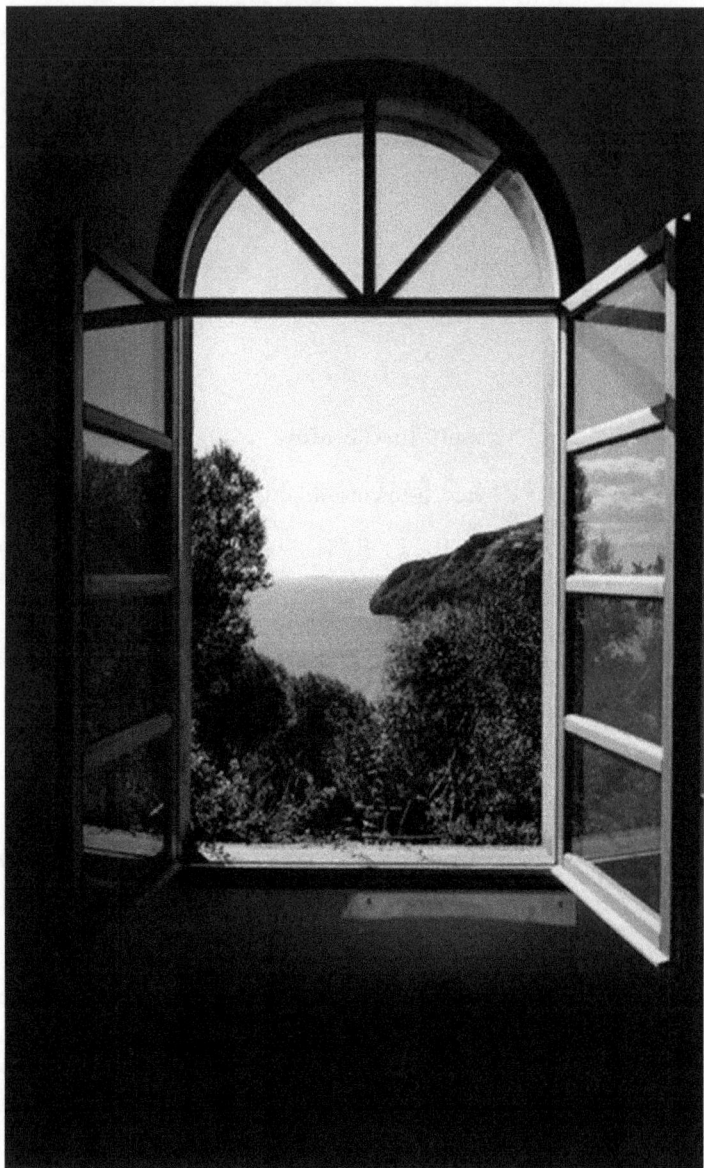

open window —
the post-its
flutter too

so early in spring —
a green leaf sticks to
the sole of his shoe

sheltering in place
the computer she gives me prompts
a big thank you

pandemic days
on the park bench only
an inscribed name

self-isolating
a young girl chalks the sidewalk
DANGER ZONE

still a mystery
how they work
post-it notes

neighborhood walk —
without his notepad
he picks up a leaf

into the pail
filled with free lemons
another thank you note

fresh blueberries —
the small stain
on his writing pad

reading her note
it's over
in a flash

pandemic isolation —
recovery lies in the company
of post-its

Sunday afternoon --
I add a brief entry
to the ladybug's diary

fresh daisies --
who says I can't write
myself a love note?

trail's end —
a note tightly folded
in a dollar

winter rain --
the writing on the wall
isn't

Memorial Day --
what keeps me up
isn't legible

from one
sticky note to another
this life

Stop
Telling
Time

outdoor café —
sunlight refilling
her empty glass

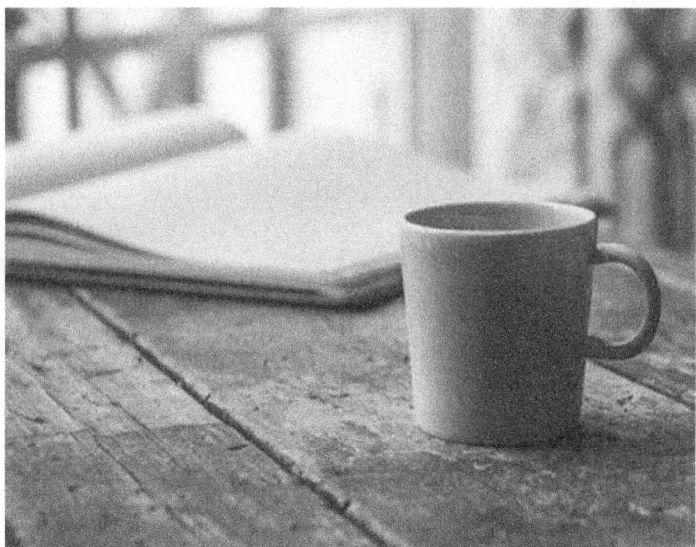

between morning tea
& morning meditation
waking up

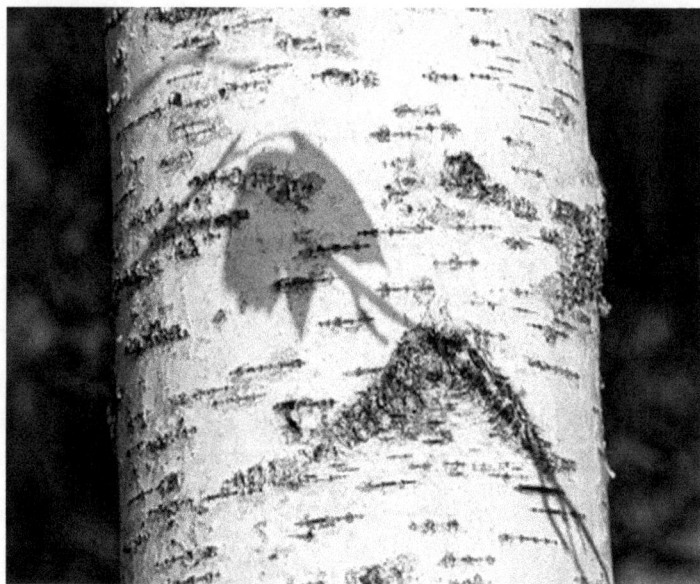

for

the

ant

up

&

down

the

birch

tree

takes

as

long

as

it

takes

fog-drenched nights
I refuse to change
the flannel pillowcases

peeling potatoes
I don't need to make
a difference anymore

tossing celery
into the soup pot
are you ready to die?

undeterred by the cold
a curious boy enchanted
with his own breath

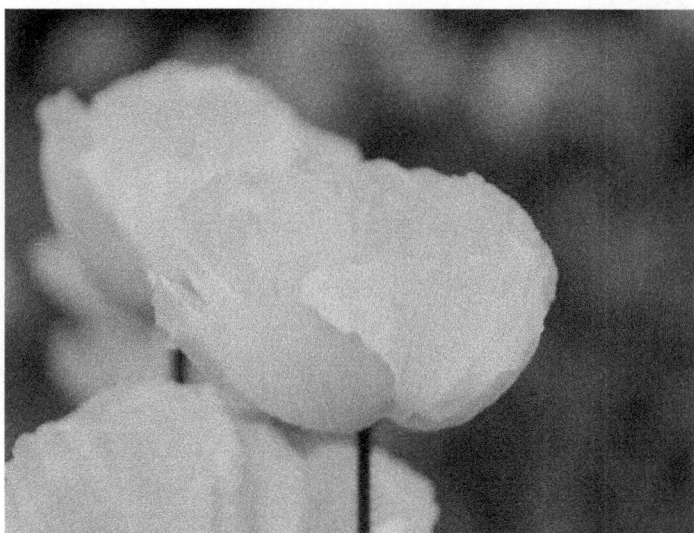

in the street too

just outside the moment

a neighbor's poppy

shipping carton --
I crumple up
yesterday's news

the living room clock
stops telling time
so do I

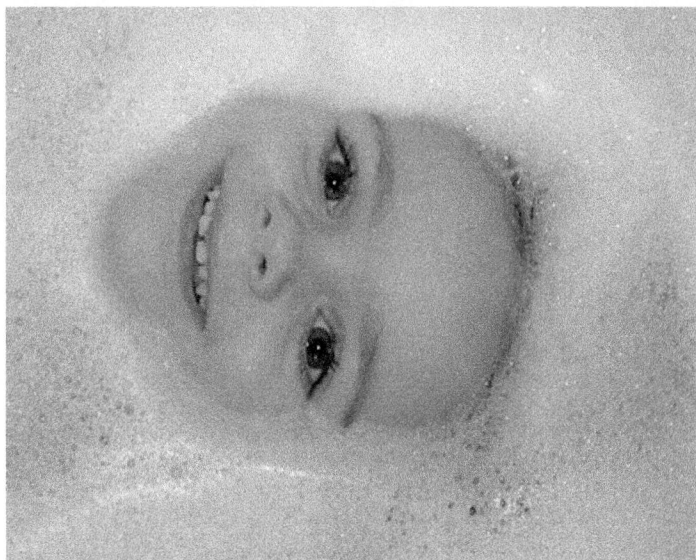

in the bathtub reading the bubbles

that nonstop monarch. . .
I frame my mother's last
birthday card

old to-do list
atop my dad's dresser
untouched

the strawberry plant
comes back to life
a second time here

late May
the message
a fading poppy drops

buy more batteries
not for the flashlight,
for me

vista point --
my family so far away
I hold them right here[1]

lockdown --
my friends & I get
a little closer

a stone in my shoe
free of time
free of meaning

~ *In Memory of John Welwood*[2]

when words
only reach the canyon
of her heart

rest stop --
she wonders where
the time went

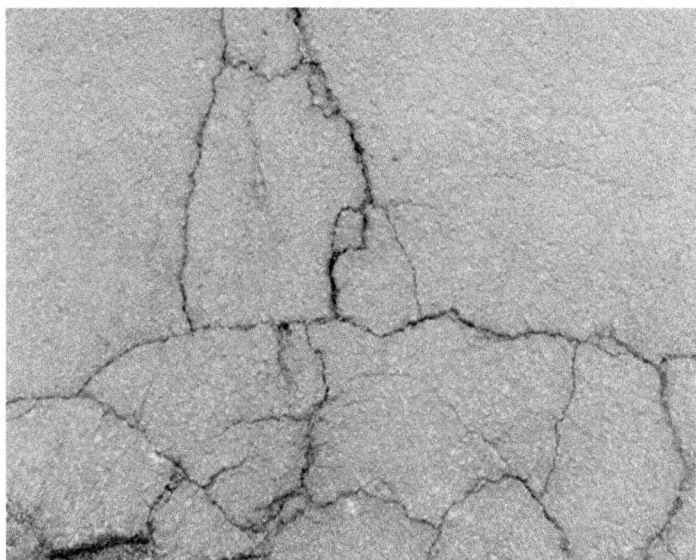

cracks in the road --
they too are another
reminder

drip drip drip
not the kitchen faucet
the moments of my day

out of ink
I pick up a stick
& etch the sky

nearly unseen
the raccoon slips down the grate
out of time

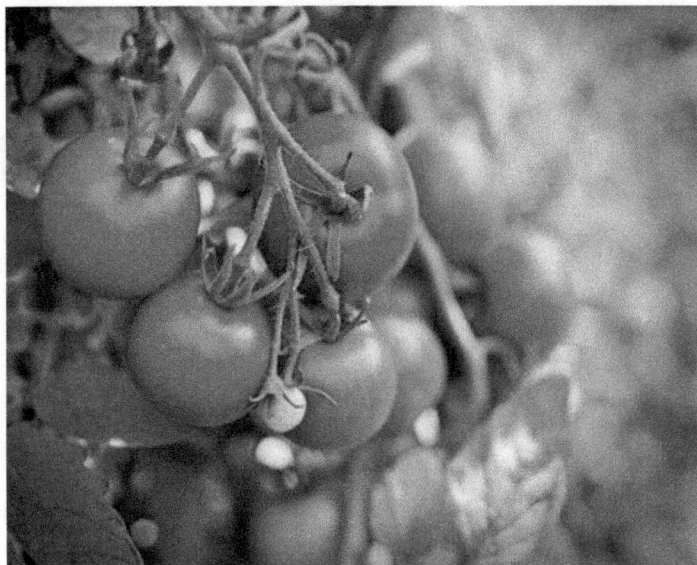

planting tomatoes
the moment yields
a little room

just when I thought
nothing was going on
molehills

this aging body --
each new condition
comes with a warning

sky pilot --
how high can you fly
in the old age home

~*after Eric Burden*

Unfinished

monkey mind --
its sights already set
on the afterlife

~after Natalie Goldberg

dishes drying
on the dish rack
I need a dare

the book

dedicated to my mentor

a few months too late

~ *In Memory of Dan B. Wile*

have you noticed. . .
every breath is the first
and the last

drifting off --
I find myself
in the corpse pose

curbside --
in the original box
her unfinished puzzle

no life
is ever fully complete
a blooming and dying rose

GIVE PEACE A CHANCE

so many stars. . .
even if gunned down
we all shine on

~ In Honor of John Lennon

one last post-it
left blank except
for. . .

Notes

1. My siblings and their families live on the East Coast while I have lived in northern California since 1982.

2. Many times in therapy I have pointed out that the alternative to meaning is not only meaninglessness but *meaning-freeness*, a thought-provoking term I learned from John Welwood in a paper he wrote, "Exploring Mind: Form, Emptiness, and Beyond." John Welwood, ed. *The Meeting of the Ways: Explorations in East/West Psychology*. New York, NY: Shocken Books, 1979.

*Put away the book, the descriptions,
the traditions, the authority, and take
the journey of self-discovery.*

~ J. Krishnamurti, *Commentaries on Living*, Third Series

www.ingramcontent.com/pod-product-compliance
Lightning Source LLC
Chambersburg PA
CBHW060807050426
42449CB00008B/1576